folksongs
and ballads
popular in
ireland

Volume 2

collected, arranged
and edited by
john Loesberg

SWANS SING BEFORE THEY DIE, — T'WERE NO BAD THING
SHOULD CERTAIN PERSONS DIE BEFORE THEY SING.

S.T. Coleridge

ACKNOWLEDGEMENTS

For checking the musical material thanks are due to
Florence Linehan of the Cork School of Music and to
the staff of the Cork City Library for their assistance.

The editor is indebted to Messrs Walton, Dublin for
their permission to include   The Whistlin' Gypsy and
Westminster Music , London for the inclusion of
'Avondale' by Dominic Behan © 1964, Coda Music.

ISBN 0 946005 01 X

ALL ADAPTATIONS AND ARRANGEMENTS

OSSIAN PUBLICATIONS
21 IONA GREEN, CORK, IRELAND

PRINTED BY LEE PRESS, CORK

THE RAGGLE TAGGLE GYPSIES

Three gyp-sies stood at the cas- tle gate, They sang so high, they sang so low, The la-dy sat in her cham- ber late, Her heart it melt- ed a- way as snow.

They sang so sweet, they sang so shrill,
That fast her tears began to flow
And she laid down her silken gown
Her golden rings and all her show.

She pluck-ed off her high-heeled shoes,
A-made of Spanish leather, O
She went in the street with her bare, bare feet;
All out in the wind and weather, O.

O saddle to me my milk-white steed,
And go and fetch my pony, O
That I may ride and seek my bride,
Who is gone with the raggle taggle gypsies, O.

O he rode high and he rode low,
He rode through wood and copses too,
Until he came to an open field,
And there he espied his lady, O.

What makes you leave your house and land
Your golden treasures for to go
What makes you leave your new-wedded lord,
To follow the raggle taggle gypsies, O.

What care I for my house and my land
What care I for my treasure, O
What care I for my newly-wedded lord,
I'm off with the raggle taggle gypsies, O.

Last night you slept on a goose-feather bed,
With the sheets turned down so bravely, O
And to-night you'll sleep in a cold open field,
Along with the raggle taggle gypsies, O.

What care I for a goose-feather bed
With the sheet turned down so bravely, O
For to-night I shall sleep in a cold open field,
Along with the raggle taggle gypsies, O.

ALTERNATIVE CHORDSHAPES :
Capo in second box
Bm = Am, F#m = Em, G = F.

1

the shores of amerikay

♩. = 60

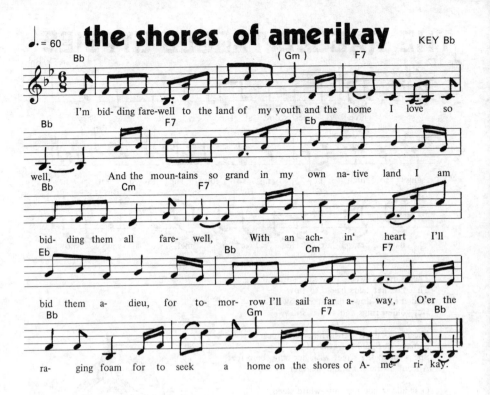

I'm bid- ding fare-well to the land of my youth and the home I love so well, And the moun-tains so grand in my own na- tive land I am bid- ding them all fare- well, With an ach- in' heart I'll bid them a- dieu, for to-mor- row I'll sail far a- way, O'er the ra- ging foam for to seek a home on the shores of A- me- ri- kay.

It's not for the want of employment I'm going
It's not for the love of fame
That fortune bright may shine over me,
And give me a glorious name
It's not for the want of employment I'm going
O'er the weary and stormy sea,
But to seek a home for my own true love,
On the shores of Amerikay.

And when I'm bidding my last farewell,
The tears like rain will blind
To think of my friends in my own native land
And the home I'm leaving behind.
But if I'm to die in a foreign land
And be buried so far away,
No fond mother's tears will be shed o'er my grave,
On the shores of Amerikay.

ALTERNATIVE CHORDSHAPES :
Capo in third box
Bb = G, Gm = Em, F7 = D7, Cm = Am, Eb = C.

PEGGY GORDON

♩ = 126

Oh, Peg- gy Gor- don, you are my dar-ling, Come sit you down u- pon my knee and tell to me The ve- ry rea- son Why I am sligh- ted so by thee.

I wish I was in some lonesome valley,
Where womankind cannot be found,
Where the little birds sing upon the branches,
And every moment a different sound.

Oh, Peggy Gordon, you are my darling,
Come sit you down upon my knee,
And tell to me the very reason,
Why I am slighted so by thee.

I'm so in love that I can't deny it,
My heart lies smothered in my breast,
But it's not for you to let the world know it,
A troubled mind can know no rest.

I put my head to a cask of brandy,
It was my fancy, I do declare,
For when I'm drinking I'm always thinking,
And wishing Peggy Gordon was here.

I KNOW MY LOVE

I know my love by her way of walk- ing and I know my love by her way of talk- ing and I know my love by her suit of blue but if my love leaves me what will I do ? And yet she cries ' I love him the best. But a troub- led mind sure can know no rest , And yet she cries Bon- ny boys are few, Yet if my love leaves me, what will I do ?

There is a dance house in Mardyke,
And 'tis there my dear love goes every night;
And he takes a strange girl all on his knee,
And don't you think but it troubles me.

If my love knew I could wash and wring,
And if my love knew I could weave and spin,
I could make a suit all of the finest kind,
But the want of money, it leaves me behind.

ACCORDIONS

from

5/11.

4

THE HOLY GROUND

♩ = 126

KEY C

A- dieu, my fair young mai- den, A thous- and times a- dieu we must bid fare- well to the Ho- ly Ground and the girls that we love true. We will sail the salt sea o- ver and re- turn a- gain for sure, To seek the girls who wait for us in the Ho- ly Ground once more, FINE GIRL YOU ARE, You're the girl that I a- dore And still I live in hopes to see the Ho- ly Ground once more FINE GIRL YOU ARE.

Oh the night was dark and stormy,
You scarce could see the moon,
And our good old ship was tossed about,
And her rigging was all torn;
With her seams agape and leaky,
With her timbers dozed and old,
And still I live in hopes to see,
The Holy Ground once more.

And now the storm is over,
And we are safe on shore,
Let us drink a health to the Holy Ground
And the girls that we adore;
We will drink strong ale and porter
Till we make the taproom roar
And when our money all is spent
We will go to sea for more.

MRS. MC. GRATH

♩ = 100 KEY G

'Oh, mis-sus Mc Grath,' the ser-geant said 'Would you like to make a sol-dier out of your son Ted, With a scar-let coat and a big cocked hat, now mis-sus Mc Grath would-n't you like that? Wid yer too- ri- aa, fol- the did- dle aa, too- ri- oo- ri- oo- ri- aa, Wid yer too- ri- aa, fol- the did- dle aa, too- ri- oo- ri- oo- ri- aa.

So Mrs. Mc. Grath lived on the sea-shore,
For the space of seven long years or more
Till she saw a big ship sailing into the bay,
'Here's my son Ted, wisha, clear the way'.

'Oh captain dear, where have you been,
Have you been sailing on the Mediterreen,
Or have you any tidings of my son Ted,
Is the poor boy living, or is he dead?'

Then up comes Ted without any legs
And in their place he has two wooden pegs.
She kissed him a dozen times or two,
Saying, 'Holy Moses, 'tisn't you'.

'Oh then were you drunk or were you blind
That yeh left yer two fine legs behind,
Or was it walking upon the sea
Wore yer two fine legs from the knees away?'.

'Oh no I wasn't drunk or blind,
When I left my two fine legs behind
For a cannonball on the fifth of May
Took my two fine legs from the knees away'.

'Oh then Teddy me boy', the widow cried,
'Yer two fine legs were yer mammy's pride
Them stumps of a tree wouldn't do at all,
Why didn't you run from the big cannonball ?'.

All foreign wars I do proclaim
Between Don John and the King of Spain
And by herrins I'll make them rue the time
That they swept the legs of a child of mine'.

Oh then if I had you back again,
I'd never let you go to fight the King of Spain
For I'd rather have my Ted as he used to be
Than the King of France and his whole Navy'.

An English cartoon called
'Manning the Navy' showing a
press gang at work.

I'm a rover and seldom sober

♩ = 84   KEY F

I'm a ro- ver and sel- dom so- ber, I'm a
ro- ver of high de- gree, It's when I'm drink- ing I'm
al- ways think- ing how to gain my love's com- pa- ny.

Though the night be as dark as dungeon
Not a star to be seen above
I will be guided without a stumble
Into the arms of my own true love.

He stepped up to her bedroom window
Kneeling gently upon a stone
He rapped at her bedroom window
'Darling dear, do you lie alone ?'.

It's only me your own true lover
Open the door and let me in
For I have come on a long journey
And I'm near drenched to the skin.

She opened the door with the greatest pleasure
She opened the door and she let him in
They both shook hands and embraced eachother
Until the morning they lay as one.

The cocks were crawing, the birds were whistling
The streams they ran free about the brae,
Remember lass, I'm a ploughman laddie,
And the farmer I must obey'.

Now my love, I must go and leave thee
And though the hills they are high above
I will climb them with greater pleasure,
Since I've been in the arms of my love.

THE BLACK VELVET BAND

♩= 66

KEY E

As I went walk- ing down broad- way, not in-
A watch she pulled out of her pock- et and

ten- ding to stay ve- ry long I
slipped it right in- to my hand On the

met with a fro- lick- some dam- sel as she came a- trip- ping a-
ve- ry first day that I met her ; bad luck to the black vel- vet

long. Her eyes they shone like dia- monds, you'd
band.

think she was queen of the land With her hair thrown o- ver her

shoul- der tied up with a black vel- vet band.

'Twas in the town of Tralee an apprentice to trade I was bound
With a-plenty of bright amusement to see the days go round
Till misfortune and trouble came over me, which caused me to
                                    stray from my land,
Far away from my friends and relations, to follow the
                                    Black Velvet Band.

Before the judge and the jury the both of us had to appear,
And a gentleman swore to the jewellery- the case against us
                                    was clear,
For seven years transportation right unto Van Dieman's Land
Far away from my friends and relations, to follow her
                                    Black Velvet Band.

Oh all you brave young Irish lads, a warning take by me,
Beware of the pretty young damsels that are knocking around in
                                    Tralee
They'll treat you to whiskey and porter, until you're unable to stand
And before you have time for to leave them, you are unto Van
9   Dieman's Land.

FOLLOW ME UP TO CARLOW

Lift Mac Ca- hir Og your face brood- ing o'er the
Grey said vic- to- ry was sure soon the fire- brand

old dis- grace, that black Fitz- Wil- liam stormed your place and
he'd se- cure; un- till he met at Glen- ma- lure ————

drove you to the Fern | Curse and swear Lord Kil- dare,
Feach Mac Hugh O' Byrne. | Now Fitz- Wil- liam, have a care

Feagh will do what Feach will dare - Up with hal- bert
Fal- len is your star, low.

Out with sword, On we go for by the Lord

Feach Mac Hugh has gi- ven his word, — Fol- low me up to Car- low.

See the swords of Glen Imayle, flashing o'er the English Pale
See all the children of the Gael, beneath O' Byrne's banners
Rooster of the fighting stock, would you let a Saxon cock
Crow out upon an Irish rock, fly up and teach him manners.

From Tassagart to Clonmore, flows a stream of Saxon gore
Och, great is Rory Oge O' More, at sending loons to Hades.
White is sick and Lane is fled, now for black Fitzwilliam's head
We'll send it over, dripping red, to Liza and the ladies.

THE BLACKSMITH

♩ = 112

KEY Dm

A black-smith cour-ted me, nine months and bet-ter

He fair-ly won my heart, wrote me a let-ter

With his ham-mer in his hand, he looked so cle-ver

And if I was with my love I'd live for-ev-er.

And where is my love gone, with his cheeks like roses
And his good black billycock on, decked with primroses
I'm afraid the scorching sun will shine and burn his beauty
And if I was with my love, I'd do my duty.

Strange news is come to town, strange news is carried,
Strange news flies up and down that my love is married
I wish them both much joy, though they don't hear me
And may God reward him well, for slighting of me.

What did you promise, love, when you sat beside me
You said you would marry me and not deny me
'If I said I'd marry you, it was only for to try you,
So bring your witness love, and I'll ne'er deny you'.

Oh witness have I none, save God Almighty
And He'll reward you well for the slighting of me
Her lips grew pale and white, it made her poor heart tremble
To think she loved one and he proved deceitful.

THE WEST'S AWAKE

KEY G

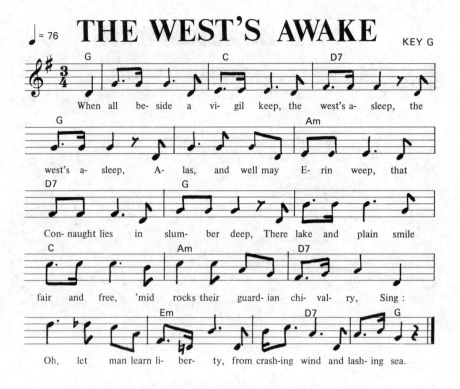

When all be- side a vi- gil keep, the west's a- sleep, the west's a- sleep, A- las, and well may E- rin weep, that Con- naught lies in slum- ber deep, There lake and plain smile fair and free, 'mid rocks their guard- ian chi- val- ry, Sing : Oh, let man learn li- ber- ty, from crash-ing wind and lash- ing sea.

That chainless wave and lovely land
Freedom and Nationhood demand
Be sure the great God never planned
For slumb'ring slaves a home so grand
And long a proud and haughty race
Honour'd and sentinell'd the place
Sing, Oh, not e'en their sons' disgrace
Can quite destroy their glory's trace

For often in O'Connors van
To triumph dashed each Connacht clan
And fleet as deer the Normans ran
Through Curlew's Pass and Ardrahan;
And later times saw deeds as brave
And glory guards Clanricarde's grave;
Sing, Oh, they died their land to save
At Aughrim's slopes and Shannon's wave.

And if, when all a vigil keep
The West's asleep, the West's asleep
Alas and well may Erin weep
That Connaught lies in slumber deep;
But hark, a voice like thunder spake
The West's awake, the West's awake
Sing, Oh, Hurrah, let England quake
We'll watch till death for Erin's sake.

The Long Song Seller. Mayhew's *London Labour and the London Poor*.

DANNY BOY

KEY C

Oh, Dan- ny boy, the pipes, the pipes are cal- ling, From glen to glen and down the moun-tain- side, The sum- mer's gone and all the ro- ses fal- ling, 'Tis you 'tis you must go and I must bide, But come ye back when sum-mer's in the mea- dow, Or when the val- ley's hushed and white with snow, 'Tis I'll be there in sun- shine or in sha- dow, Oh Dan- ny boy, Oh Dan- ny boy I love you so.

And when you come and all the flowers are dying
If I am dead- as dead I well may be
Ye'll come and find a place where I am lying
And kneel and say an Ave there for me;
And I shall hear though soft your tread above me,
And all my grave shall warmer, sweeter be,
For you will bend and tell me that you love me
And I shall live in peace, until you come to me.

THE WHISTLIN' GYPSY ROVER

The gyp- sy ro- ver came o- ver the hill,
How- dy do, how- dy do dah — day,

down through the val- ley so sha- dy, He
how- dy do how- dy day ——— He

whist- led and he sang till the green- woods rang and
whist- led and he sang till the green- woods rang and

he won the heart of a la- dy.
he won the heart of a la- dy.

She left her father's castle gate,
She left her own true lover
She left her servants and her estate
To follow the gypsy rover

Her father saddled up his fastest steed
Roamed the valleys all over
He sought his daughter at great speed
And the whistlin' gypsy rover.

He came at last to a mansion fine
Down by the river Clady
And there was music and there was wine
For the gypsy and his lady.

He is no gypsy, father ' said she
'But lord of these lands all over
And I shall stay till my dying day
With my whistlin' gypsy rover '.

15

the beggerman's song

♩ = 116

KEY D

I am a lit- tle beg- gar- man and beg- ging I have been, for three score years in this lit- tle isle of green, I'm known a- long the Lif- fey from the Ba- sin to the Zoo, and ev'- ry- bo- dy calls me by the name of John- ny Dhu— Of all trades a- go- ing, sure the beg- ging is the best, for when a man is ti- red he can sit him down and rest, He can beg for his din- ner, he has noth- ing else to do but to slip a- round the cor- ner with his ould ri- ga- doo.

I slept in a barn one night in Currabawn,
A shocking wet night it was but I slept until the dawn;
There was holes in the roof and the raindrops coming through,
And the rats and the cats were all playing peek-a-boo.
Who did I waken but the woman of the house
With her white-spotted apron and her fine gingham blouse;
She began to get exited and all I said was ' Boo !
Sure, don't be afraid at all, 'tis only Johnny Dhu '.

I met a little girl when a-walking out one day,
'Good-morrow, little flaxen-haired girl ' I did say;
'Good-morrow, little beggarman, and how do you do,
With your rags and your tags and your ould rigadoo'.
'I'll buy a pair of leggings and a collar and a tie,
And a nice young lady I'll go courting by and by;
I'll buy a pair of goggles and I'll colour them with blue,
And an old-fashioned lady I will make her too'.

So all along the highroad with my bag upon my back
Over the fields with my bulging heavy sack;
With holes in my shoes and my toes a-peeping through,
Singing ' Skin-a-ma-link-a-doodle with my ould rigadoo,
Oh I must be going to bed, for it's getting late at night,
The fire is all raked and now 'tis out the light;
For now you've heard the story of my ould rigadoo,
So good-bye and God be with you, from old Johnny Dhu.'

AVONDALE

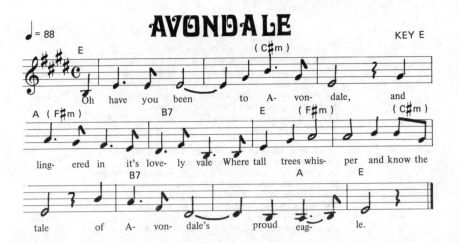

Oh have you been to A-von-dale, and ling-ered in it's love-ly vale Where tall trees whis-per and know the tale of A-von-dale's proud eag-le.

Where pride and ancient glory fade,
So was the land where he was laid
Like Christ was thirty pieces paid
For Avondale's proud eagle.

Long years that green and lovely vale
Has nursed Parnell, her grandest Gael
And curse the land that has betrayed
Fair Avondale's proud eagle.

CHARLES STUART PARNELL, M.P., PRESIDENT of the IRISH LAND LEAGUE, ADDRESSING A MEETING.

NORA

♩ = 104

The vio- lets were scent-ing the woods, No- ra, dis- play- ing their charm to the bee, When I first said I loved on- ly you, No- ra and you said you loved on- ly me. The chest- nut blooms gleamed through the glade, No- ra, a ro- bin sang loud from a tree, When I first said I loved on- ly you, No- ra, and you said you loved on- ly me.

The golden-robed daffodils shone, Nora,
And danced in the breeze on the lea,
When I first said I loved only you, Nora,
And you said you loved only me.

The trees, birds and bees sang a song, Nora,
Of happier transports to be,
When I first said I loved only you, Nora,
And you said you loved only me.

KELLY THE BOY FROM KILLANNE

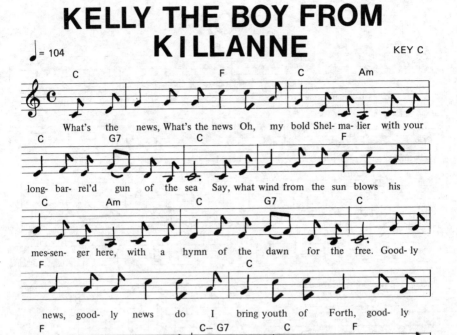

♩ = 104

What's the news, What's the news Oh, my bold Shel- ma- lier with your long- bar- rel'd gun of the sea Say, what wind from the sun blows his mes-sen- ger here, with a hymn of the dawn for the free. Good- ly news, good- ly news do I bring youth of Forth, good- ly news you shall hear, Bar- gy men. For the boys march at dawn from the south to the north, led by Kel- ly the boy from Kil- lane.

Tell me who is the giant with the gold curling hair
He who rides at the head of your band
Seven feet is his height, with some inches to spare,
And he looks like a king in command
'Oh me boys, that's the pride of the bold Shelmaliers,
'Mongst our greatest of heroes, a Man.
Fling your beavers aloft and give three rousing cheers
For John Kelly, the Boy from Killanne.

Enniscorthy's in flames and old Wexford is won
And the Barrow tomorrow we cross
On a hill o'er the town we have planted a gun
That will batter the gateways to Ross
All the Forth men and Bargey men march o'er the heath
With brave Harvey to lead on the van;
But the foremost of all in that grim gap of death
Will be Kelly, the Boy from Killane.

But the gold sun of freedom grew darkened at Ross
And it set by the Slaney's red waves
And poor Wexford stripped naked, hung high on a cross
With her heart pierced by traitors and slaves
Glory O, Glory O to her brave sons who died
For the cause of the long-downtrodden man
Glory O to Mount Leinster's own darling and pride
Dauntless Kelly, the Boy of Killane.

the banks of the ohio

KEY F

♩= 130

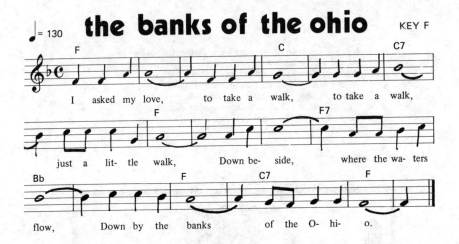

I asked my love, to take a walk, to take a walk, just a lit- tle walk, Down be- side, where the wa- ters flow, Down by the banks of the O- hi- o.

And only say that you'll be mine
And in no other arms will twine
Down beside where the waters flow
Down by the banks of the Ohio.

I held a knife against her breast
As unto my arm she pressed
She cried 'Oh Willie, don't murder me
I'm not prepared for eternity'.

I started home 'tween twelve and one
I cried my God, what have I done
Killed the only girl I loved
Because she wouldn't be my dove.

22

MAIDS WHEN YOU'RE YOUNG

KEY G

An old man came cour-ting me, hey ding- a doo- rum dah,
–– got no fal- oo- doo- rum, fal did- dle oo- doo- rum,

An old man came cour-ting me me be- ing young, An
He's got no fal- oo- doo- rum, fal did- dle day, He's

old man came cour- ting me all for his wife to be
got no fal- oo- doo- rum, lost his ding doo- ree- um,

Maids when you're young ne- ver wed an old man. For he's
Maids when you're young ne- ver wed an old man. *Chorus.*

When this old man comes to bed, hey ding a doorum dah
When this old man comes to bed, me being young
When this old man comes to bed, he lays like a lump of lead
Maids when you're young never wed an old man.

When this old man goes to sleep, hey ding a doorum dah
When this old man goes to sleep, me being young
When this old man goes to sleep, out of bed I do creep
Into the arms of a handsome young man.

I wish this old man would die, hey ding a doorum dah
I wish this old man would die, me being young
I wish this old man would die, I'd make the money fly
Girls for your sakes never wed an old man.

A young man is my delight, hey ding a doorum dah
A young man is my delight, me being young
A young man is my delight, he'll kiss you day and night
Maids when you're young never wed an old man.

THE GALWAY RACES

♩ = 120

KEY A

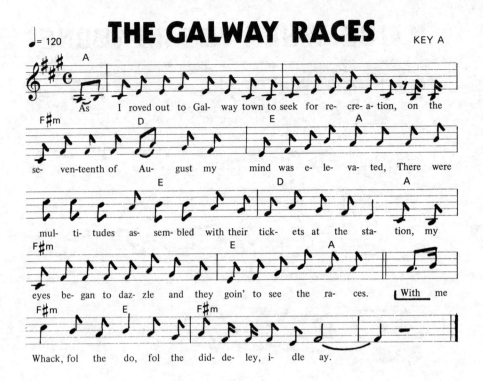

As I roved out to Galway town to seek for recreation, on the seventeenth of August my mind was elevated, There were multitudes assembled with their tickets at the station, my eyes began to dazzle and they goin' to see the races. With me Whack, fol the do, fol the did-deley, idle ay.

There were passengers from Limerick and passengers from Nenagh
And passengers from Dublin and sportsmen from Tipp'rary
There were passengers from Kerry and all the quarters of the nation
And our member, Mr Hasset for to join the Galway Blazers.

There were multitudes from Aran and members from New Quay shore
The boys from Connemara and the Clare unmarried maidens
There were people from Cork city who were loyal, true and faithful
That brought home Fenian prisoners from dying in foreign nations

It's there you'll see confectioners with sugarsticks and dainties
The lozenges and oranges, the lemonade and raisins
The gingerbread and spices to accommodate the ladies
And a big crubeen for threepence to be picking while you're able.

It's there you'll see the gamblers, the thimbles and the garters
And the sporting Wheel of Fortune with the four and twenty quarters
There were others without scruple pelting wattles at poor Maggy
And her father well contented and he looking at his daughter.

ALTERNATIVE CHORDSHAPES :
Capo in second box
A = G, F#m = Em, E = D.

24

It's there you'll see the pipers and the fiddlers competing
And the nimble-footed dancers and they tripping on the daisies
There were others crying 'Cigars and lights and bills of all the races
With the colours of the jockeys and the prize and horses' ages '.

It's there you'd see the jockeys and they mounted on most stately
The pink and blue, the red and green, the emblem of our nation
When the bell was rung for starting all the horses seemed impatient
I thought they never stood on ground, their speed was so amazing.

There was half a million people there of all denominations
The Catholic, the Protestant, the Jew and Presbyterian
There was yet no animosity, no matter what persuasion
But failte and hospitality inducing fresh acquaintance.

SAM HALL

♩ = 120

Oh, my name it is Sam Hall, chim-ney sweep, chim-ney sweep, Oh, my name it is Sam Hall, chim-ney sweep, Oh, my name it is Sam Hall and I've robbed both rich and small, And my neck will pay for all, When I die, when I die, And my neck will pay for all when I die.

Oh they took me to Coote Hill in a cart, in a cart
Oh they took me to Coote Hill in a cart
Oh they took me to Coote Hill and 'twas there I made my will
For the best of friends must part, so must I, so must I,
For the best of friends must part, so must I.

Up the ladder I did grope, that's no joke, that's no joke
Up the ladder I did grope and the hangman pulled the rope
And ne'er a word I spoke, tumbling down, tumbling down
And ne'er a word I spoke tumbling down.

Oh my name it is Sam Hall, chimney sweep, chimney sweep
Oh my name it is Sam Hall, chimney sweep
Oh my name it is Sam Hall, and I've robbed both rich and small
And my neck will pay for all when I die, when I die
And my neck will pay for all when I die.

boston city

♩. = 60

I was born in Bos- ton ci- ty boys, a place you all know well Brought up by ho- nest pa- rents, the truth to you I'll tell Brought up by hon- est pa- rents, and raised most ten- der- ly, Till I be- came a sport- ing blade at the age of twen- ty three.

My character it was taken and I was sent to jail
My parents thought to bail me out, but they found it all in vain;
The jury found me guilty, and the clerk he wrote it down
The judge he passed my sentence and I was sent to Charlestown.

I see my aged father and he standing by the Bar
Likewise my aged mother and she tearing off her hair
The tearing of her old grey locks and the tears came mingled down
Saying ' John, my son, what have you done, that you're bound for
                                              Charlestown.

There's a girl in Boston city, boys, a place you all know well
And if e'er I get my liberty, it's with her I will dwell
If e'er I get my liberty, bad company I will shun
The robbing of the Munster bank, and the drinking of rum.

You lads that are at liberty, should keep it while you can
Don't roam the street by night or day, or break the laws of man
For if you do you're sure to rue and become a lad like me
A-serving up your twenty-one years, in the Royal Artillery.

THE NIGHTINGALE

From out of his knapsack he took a fine fiddle
And he played her such merry tunes that you ever did hear
And he played her such merry tunes that the valley did ring
And they both sat down together to hear the nightingale sing.

O soldier, o soldier will you marry me
O no said the soldier, That never can be
For I have my own wife at home in my own counteree
And she is the sweetest little thing that you ever did see.

Now I'm off to India for seven long years
Drinking wines and strong whiskey instead of cool beers;
And if ever I return again it'll be in the spring
And we'll both sit down together and hear the nightingale sing.

An Irish Jig.

MY LAGAN LOVE

♩ = 88

Where La- gan stream sings lull- a- bye, there blows a li- ly fair,
the twi- light gleam is in in her eye, the night is on her hair,
And like a love- sick len- an- shee, she hath my heart in thrall;
Nor life I owe, nor li- ber- ty, for love is lord of all.

And often when the beetle's horn
Hath lulled the eye to sleep,
I steal unto her shieling lorn
And thro' the dooring peep;
There .on the cricket's singing stone
She stirs the bog-wood fire,
And hums in sad, sweet undertone
The song of heart's desire.

Her welcome like her love for me
Is from the heart within
Her warm kiss is felicity
That knows no taint or sin;
When she was only fairy small
Her gentle mother died
But true love keeps her memory warm
By Lagan's silver side.

IRISH WAR PIPER.

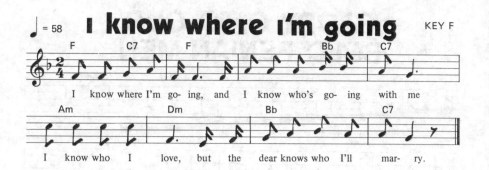

I know where I'm going

♩ = 58　　　KEY F

I know where I'm go-ing, and I know who's go-ing with me
I know who I love, but the dear knows who I'll mar-ry.

I'll have stockings of silk
Shoes of fine green leather,
Combs to buckle my hair
And a ring for every finger.

Feather beds are soft
Painted rooms are bonny;
But I'd leave them all
To go with my love Johnny.

Some say he's dark
I say he's bonny,
He's the flower of them all
My handsome, coaxing Johnny.

I know where I'm going
I know who's going with me
I know who I love
But the dear knows who I'll marry.

GLORY O, TO OUR BOLD FENIAN MEN

KEY Dm

♩ = 108

A- down by the glen- side I met an old wo- man, a-
pluck- ing young net- tles nor saw I was co- ming, I
list- ened a while, to the song she was hum- ming,
Glo- ry- O, Glo- ry- O, to the Bold Fe- nian Men.

'Tis fifty long years since I saw the moon beamin'
On strong manly forms, on eyes with hope gleamin'
I see them again, sure, thro' all my sad dreamin'
Glory O, Glory O, to the Bold Fenian Men.

When I was a girl their marching and drillin'
Awoke in the glenside sounds awesome and thrillin'
They loved poor old Ireland, to die they were willin'
Glory O, Glory O, to the Bold Fenian Men.

Some died by the glenside, some died mid the stranger;
And wise men have told us their cause was a failure;
But they stood by old Ireland, and never feared danger,
Glory O, Glory O, to the Bold Fenian Men.

I passed on my way, God be praised that I met her;
Be my life long or short I shall never forget her.
We may have had good men, but we'll never have better,
Glory O, Glory O, to the Bold Fenian Men.

CARRIGDHOUN

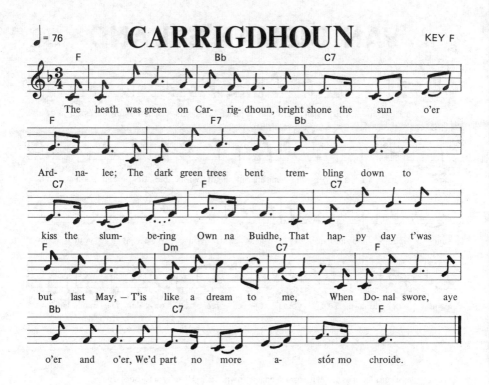

♩ = 76   KEY F

The heath was green on Car- rig- dhoun, bright shone the sun o'er Ard- na- lee; The dark green trees bent trem- bling down to kiss the slum- be-ring Own na Buidhe, That hap- py day t'was but last May, — T'is like a dream to me, When Do- nal swore, aye o'er and o'er, We'd part no more a- stór mo chroide.

On Carrig Dhoun the heath is brown
The clouds are dark o'er Ard-na-Lee;
And many a stream comes rushing down,
To swell the angry Own-na-Buidhe.
The moaning blast is sweeping past,
Through many a leafless tree;
And I'm alone, for he is gone,
My hawk has flown, ochone mo chroidhe.

Soft April showers and bright May flowers
Will bring the summer back again;
But will they bring me back the hours,
I spent with my brave Donal then
There's but a chance- he's gone to France,
To wear the Fleur-de-Lis,
But I'll follow you, my Donal Dhu,
For still I'm true to you mo chroide.

BUYE the dry Turf, buye Turf;
buye the dry Turf—Here's the dry
Bog-a-Wood.—Here's the Chips to light
the Fire; Maids!

ALTERNATIVE CHORDSHAPES :
Capo in third box
F = D, Bb = G, C7 = A7, Dm = Bm, F7 = D7.

33

VAN DIEMAN'S LAND

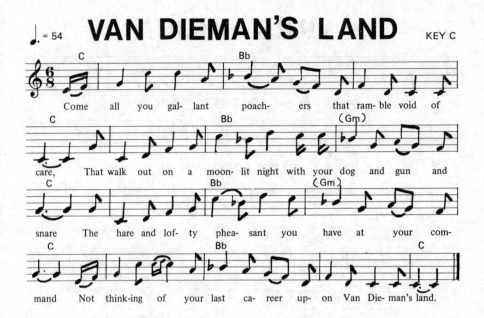

KEY C

♩. = 54

Come all you gal- lant poach- ers that ram- ble void of care, That walk out on a moon- lit night with your dog and gun and snare The hare and lof- ty phea- sant you have at your com- mand Not think-ing of your last ca- reer up- on Van Die- man's land.

Poor Thomas Brown from Nenagh town, Jack Murphy and poor Joe
Were three determined poachers as the county well does know
By the keepers of the land, my boys, one night they were trepanned
And for fourteen years transported unto Van Dieman's Land.

The first day that we landed upon that fatal shore
The planters came around us, there might be twenty-score
They ranked us off like horses and they sold us out of hand
And they yoked us to the plough, brave boys, to plough Van Dieman's Land.

The cottages we live in are built with sods of clay
We have rotten straw for bedding but we dare not say nay
Our cots we fence with firing and slumber when we can
To keep the wolves and tigers from us in Van Dieman's Land.

Oft times when I do slumber I have a pleasant dream
With my sweet girl sitting near me close to a purling stream
I am roaming through old Ireland with my true love by the hand
But awaken broken-hearted upon Van Dieman's Land.

God bless our wives and families, likewise that happy shore
That isle of sweet contentment which we ne'er shall see more
As for the wretched families, see them we seldom can
There are twenty men for one woman in Van Dieman's Land.

34

But fourteen years is a long time, that is our fatal doom
For nothing else but poaching for that is all we done
You would leave off both dog and gun and poaching, every man,
If you but knew the hardship that's in Van Dieman's Land.

Oh if I had a thousand pounds all laid out in my hand
I'd give it all for liberty if that I could command
Again to Ireland I'd return and be a happy man
And bid adieu to poaching and to Van Dieman's Land.

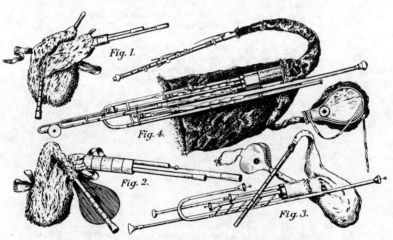

Fig. 1. Ancient Irish Bagpipe.   Fig. 2. Cuislean or Bellows Pipes.
Fig. 3. Primitive Union Pipes.   Fig. 4. Egan's Improved Union Pipes.

THE CURRAGH OF KILDARE

The win-ter it is past and the sum-mer's come at last and the small birds they sing on eve-ry tree ; Their lit-tle hearts are glad but mine is ve-ry sad, since my true love is far a-way from me.

The rose upon the brier, by the water running clear,
Gives joy to the linnet and the bee;
Their little hearts are blest, but mine is not at rest
While my true love is absent from mè.

A livery I'll wear, and I'll comb back my hair,
And in velvet so green I will appear,
And straight I will repair to the Curragh of Kildare,
For it's there I'll find tidings of my dear.

I'll wear a cap of black, with a frill around my neck,
Gold rings on my fingers I wear;
It's this I undertake, for my true lover's sake,
He resides at the Curragh of Kildare.

I would not think it strange, thus the world for to range,
If I only got tidings of my dear;
But here in Cupid's chain, if I'm bound to remain,
I would spend my whole life in despair.

My love is like the sun, that in the firmament does run;
And always proves constant and true;
But his is like the moon, that wanders up and down,
And every month is new.

All you that are in love and cannot it remove,
I pity the pains you endure;
For experience let me know, that your hearts are full of woe,
And a woe that no mortal can cure.

36

♩ = 92

the drunken sailor

What shall we do with a drunk- en sai- lor, What shall we do with a
drunk- en sai- lor, What shall we do with a drunk- en sai- lor
Ear- lye in the morn- ing.

Chorus (to the same tune as the verse above) :

Way, hey, up she rises, Way, hey, up she rises, Way, hey, up she rises,
Earlye in the morning.

Put him in the scuppers with the hosepipe on him (3 times)
Earlye in the morning

Hoist him aboard with a running bowline (3 times)
Earlye in the morning.

Put him in the brig until he's sober (3 times)
Earlye in the morning.

Make him turn to at shining bright work (3 times)
Earlye in the morning.

What shall we do with a drunken sailor (3 times)
Earlye in the morning.

THE WELL BELOW THE VALLEY

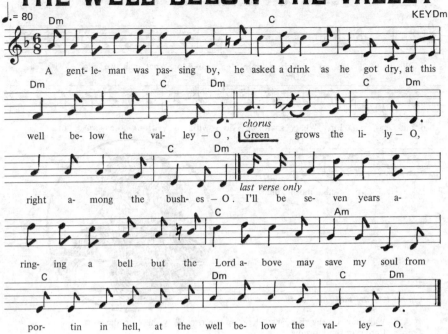

♩.= 80   KEY Dm

Dm ... **C**

A gent-le-man was pas-sing by, he asked a drink as he got dry, at this

Dm ... **C** ... **Dm**

well be-low the val-ley – O, *chorus* Green grows the li-ly – O,

C ... **Dm**

right a-mong the bush-es – O. *last verse only* I'll be se-ven years a-

C ... **Am**

ring-ing a bell but the Lord a-bove may save my soul from

C ... **Dm** ... **C** ... **Dm**

por-tin in hell, at the well be-low the val-ley – O.

She said ' My cup it overflows, if I stoop down I might fall in
At the well below the valley-o.

If your true love was passing by, you'd fill him a drink if he got dry
At the well below the valley-o.

She swore by grass, she swore by corn, that her true love was never born
At the well below the valley-o.

I say, young maid, you're swearing wrong, for five fine children
you had born
At the well below the valley-o.

If you're a man of noble fame, you'll tell me who's the father of them
At the well below the valley-o.

There was two of them by your uncle Dan, another two by
your brother John

At the well below the valley-o.

Another by your father dear at the well below the valley-o
At the well below the valley-o.

Well if you're a man of noble fame, you'll tell me what did happen
                                                  to them
At the well below the valley-o.

There was two of them buried by the stable door, another two 'neath
                                        the kitchen floor
At the well below the valley-o.

Another's buried by the well, at the well below the valley-o
At the well below the valley-o.

Well if you're a man of noble fame, you'll tell me what will
                                          happen myself
At the well below the valley-o.

You'll be seven years a-portering in hell, and seven years
                                    a-ringing a bell
At the well below the valley-o.

I'll be seven years a-ringing a bell, but the Lord above may save my soul
                                        from portin' in hell
At the well below the valley-o.

GOD SAVE IRELAND

♩ = 96   KEY A

High u- pon the gal- lows tree swung the nob- le heart- ed three, by the
venge-ful ty- rant strick- en in their bloom, but they met him face to face with the
cou- rage of the race, and they went with souls un-daun- ted to their doom.
God save Ire- land, said the he- roes, God save Ire- land, said they all, Wheth- er
on the scaf- fold high or the bat- tle- field we die, O what
mat- ter if for Ire- land dear we fall.

Girt around with cruel foes, still their courage proudly rose,
For they thought of hearts that loved them far and near;
Of the millions true and brave o'er the ocean's swelling wave;
And the friend of holy Ireland ever dear.

Climbed they up the rugged stair, rang their voices out in prayer
Then with England's fatal cord around them cast,
Close beside the gallows tree, kissed like brothers lovingly,
True to home and faith and freedom to the last.

Never till the latest day shall the memory pass away
O the gallant lives thus given for our land;
But on the cause must go amid joy or weal or woe,
Till we make our Isle a nation free and grand.

A NEW SONG CALL'D
GROGANS GROVE

As I roved out one eveing it being in the month
of May
sing fond of recreation through the fields I
took my vvay
nd for to pass some d olful time its through
the fields I off times rov'd
And there to rest my vveory limbs I sat dovvn
by Grogans grove

I had not been long there till a lovely maid had
pas'd ms by
And on that fairest creature I soon did cast a
vvishful eye
Saying vvho is she that pas'd this vvay that
do incline me f g to rove
And that veay instant moment I felt my heart
inclind to love

I arose & follovved after io see vvhat road this
fair one vvent
Still hoping that my vveary limbs vvould yield
ta me some strenth
At leath I over tok her beneath a silent purlin
stream
And there I stoo l in great surprise to gaze upon
that lovely dame

Her teeth vver like the ivory her hair a lovely
brovvn
And over her broad shoulders carelessy hung
dovvn
Her cheeks vvere like the rose her neck vvas
like the sv an
She far exceeds Diana fair or the Godness of the
Sun

ld vvish I vvas iu Derry tovvn just sitting at
my ease
And in my hand a bottle of vvine this fair maid
I vvould pl se
I vvould rove through Derry City vvith the girl
that I love
And I vvould reconcile those doleful days I sat
dovvn by Grogans Grove

41

the croppy boy

$\downarrow$ = 58   KEY G

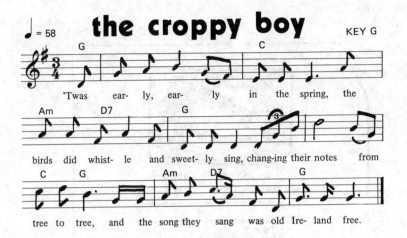

'Twas early, early in the spring, the
birds did whistle and sweetly sing, changing their notes from
tree to tree, and the song they sang was old Ireland free.

'Twas early, early on a Tuesday night
When the Yeomen cavalry gave me a fright,
To my misfortune and sad downfall
I was taken prisoner by Lord Cornwall.

'Twas in his guard-house where I was laid.
And in his parlour I was tried
My sentence passed and my spirits low,
When to New Geneva I was forced to go.

When I was marching over Wexford Hill,
Oh, who could blame me to cry my fill
I looked behind, I looked before,
But my tender mother I ne'er saw no more.

Farewell father and mother too,
And sister Mary I have none but you
And for my brother, he's all alone,
He's pointing pikes on the grinding stone.

'Twas in old Ireland this young man died
And in old Ireland his body's laid
All the good people that do pass by,
Pray the Lord have mercy on the Croppy Boy.

THE RIDDLE SONG

♩ = 80   KEY E

I gave my love a cher- ry that has no stone, I gave my love a chick- en that has no bone, I gave my love a ring that has no end, I gave my love a ba- by that's no cry- ing.

How can there be a cherry that has no stone
How can there be a chicken that has no bone
How can there be a ring that has no end
How can there be a baby that has no cryin'

A cherry when it's blooming, it has no stone
A chicken when it's pipping, it has no bone
A ring when it's rolling, it has no end
A baby when it's sleeping, has no cryin'

43

JOHNNY I HARDLY KNEW YEH

KEY Em

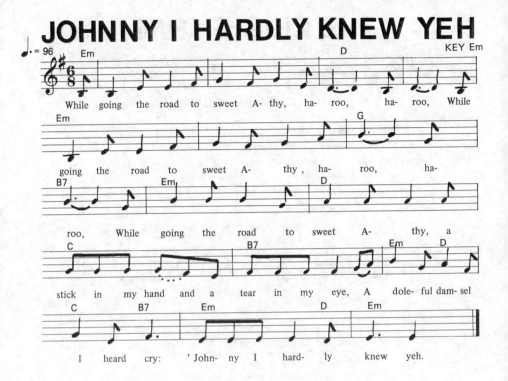

While going the road to sweet A- thy, ha- roo, ha- roo, While going the road to sweet A- thy, ha- roo, ha- roo, While going the road to sweet A- thy, a stick in my hand and a tear in my eye, A dole- ful dam- sel I heard cry: 'John- ny I hard- ly knew yeh.

Chorus (to the same tune as verse above) :

With drums and guns and guns and drums, ha-roo, ha-roo,
With drums and guns and guns and drums, ha-roo, ha-roo,
With drums and guns and guns and drums the enemy nearly slew yeh,
My darling dear you look so queer, Johnny I hardly knew yeh.

Where are the eyes that looked so mild haroo, haroo
Where are the eyes that looked so mild haroo, haroo
Where are the eyes that looked so mild,
When my poor heart you first beguiled
Why did you skedaddle from me and the child,
Johnny I hardly knew yeh.

Where are the legs with which you run haroo, haroo
Where are the legs with which you run haroo, haroo
Where are the legs with which you run,
When you went to shoulder a gun
Indeed your dancing days are done
Johnny I hardly knew yeh

It grieved my heart to see you sail haroo, haroo
It grieved my heart to see you sail haroo, haroo
It grieved my heart to see you sail,
Though from my heart you took leg-bail;
Like a cod you're doubled up head and tail
Johnny I hardly knew yeh.

44

You haven't an arm and you haven't a leg haroo, haroo
You haven't an arm and you haven't a leg haroo, haroo
You haven't an arm and you haven't a leg,
You're an eyeless, noseless, chickenless egg
You'll have to be put in a bowl to beg
Johnny I hardly knew yeh.

I'm happy for to see you home haroo, haroo
I'm happy for to see you home haroo, haroo
I'm happy for to see you home
All from the island of Sulloon
So low in the flesh so high in the bone
Johnny I hardly knew yeh.

But sad as it is to see you so haroo, haroo
But sad as it is to see you so haroo, haroo
But sad as it is to see you so,
And to think of you now as an object of woe
Your Peggy'll still keep you on as her beau;
Johnny I hardly knew yeh.

The humble Petition of us the Parliaments poore Souldiers in the

Army of Ireland, whereof many are starved already, and many dead for want of Chirurgions,

STILL I LOVE HIM

KEY C

When I was sing- le I wore a black shawl, Now that I'm
mar- ried I've noth- ing at all, Still I love him
I'll for- give him, I'll go with him wher- e- ver he goes

He stands at the corner and whistles me out
His hands in his pockets, his shirt hanging out

He bought me a handkerchief red white and blue
And then to clean windows he tore it in two.

He comes down our alley and whistles me out
And when I get out there he knocks me about.

He took me to the alehouse and bought me some stout
Before I could drink it he ordered me out.

46

the road to dundee

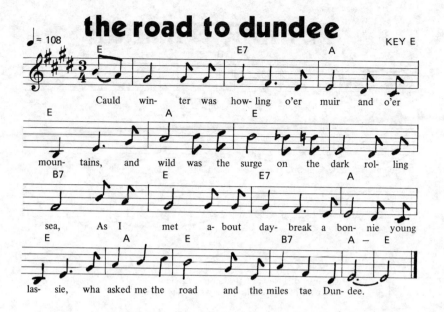

♩ = 108   KEY E

Cauld win- ter was how- ling o'er muir and o'er moun- tains, and wild was the surge on the dark rol- ling sea, As I met a- bout day- break a bon- nie young las- sie, wha asked me the road and the miles tae Dun- dee.

Said I, 'My young lassie, I canna weel tell ye,
The road and the distance I canna weel gie
But if you'll permit me tae gang a wee bittie
I'll show ye the road and the miles tae Dundee.

At once she consented and gave me her arm
Ne'er a word did I speir wha the lassie might be
She appeared like an angel in feature and form
As she walked by my side on the road tae Dundee.

At length wi' the howe of Strathmartine behin' us
An' the spires of the toon in full view we could see
She said 'Gentle sir, I can ne'er forget ye
For showing me so far on the road tae Dundee.

This ring and this purse take to prove I am grateful
And some simple token in trust ye'll gie me
Then bravely I kissed the sweet lips o' the lassie
'Ere I parted with her on the road tae Dundee.

So here's tae the lassie- I ne'er can forget her
And ilka young laddie that's listening to me
And ne'er be shy to convoy a young lassie
Though it's only to show her the road tae Dundee.

cauld = cold, muir = moor, tae = to, canna weel =
cannot well, speir wha = question who, howe =
flat tract of land, gie = give, ilka = every.

PLAISIR D'AMOUR

♩ = 112   KEY D

Plai- sir d' a- mour   ne du- re
qu'un mo- ment,   Cha- grin d'a-
mour du- re tou- te la vie.

The joys of love are but a moment long
The pain of love endures the whole night long.

Your eyes kissed mine, I saw a love in them shine,
You brought me heaven on earth, when your eyes kissed mine.

My love loves me, and all the wonders I see
A rainbow shines in my window, my love loves me.

And now he's gone, like a dream that fades into dawn,
But the world stays locked in my heartstrings, my love loves me.

Plaisir d'amour, ne dure qu'un moment,
Chagrin d'amour dure toute la vie.

48

the hills of connemara

♩ = 176

C   F   C

Gath-er up the pots and the old tin can, the mash, the

Em   F   G7   C   C7   F

corn, the bar-ley and the bran, Run like the de- vil from the ex- cise

C   G7   C

man, Keep the smoke from ri- sing, Bar- ney.

Keep your eyes well peeled today
The tall, tall men are on their way,
Searching for the mountain tay
In the Hills of Connemara.

Swing to the left and swing to the right,
The excise men will dance all night,
Drinking up the tay till the broad daylight,
In the Hills of Connemara.

A gallon for the butcher, a quart for Tom
A bottle for poor old Father Tom
To help the poor old dear along,
In the Hills of Connemara.

Stand your ground, it is too late,
The excise men are at the gate,
Glory be to Paddy, but they're drinking it nate,
In the hills of Connemara.

PADDY WORKS ON THE RAILWAY

In eigh- teen hun- dred and for- ty one, my cor- du- roy breech- es I put on, My cor- du- roy breech- es I put on, to work u- pon the rail- way, The rail- way, I'm wear- y of the rail- way, poor Pad- dy works on the rail- way.

In eighteen hundred and forty two
I didn't know what I should do,
I didn't know what I should do,
To work upon the railway.

In eighteen hundred and forty three
I took a trip across the sea
I took a trip across the sea,
To work upon the railway.

In eighteen hundred and forty four
I landed on Columbia's shore
I landed on Columbia's shore,
To work upon the railway.

In eighteen hundred and forty five
When Daniel O'Connell was alive
When Daniel O'Connell was alive,
To work upon the railway.

In eighteen hundred and forty six
I changed my trade to carrying bricks
I changed my trade to carrying bricks
To work upon the railway.

In eighteen hundred and forty seven
Poor Paddy was thinking of going to heaven
Poor Paddy was thinking of going to heaven,
To work upon the railway.

In eighteen hundred and forty eight
I learned to take my whiskey straight
I learned to take my whiskey straight
To work upon the railway.

51

THE PRATIES

♩ = 104

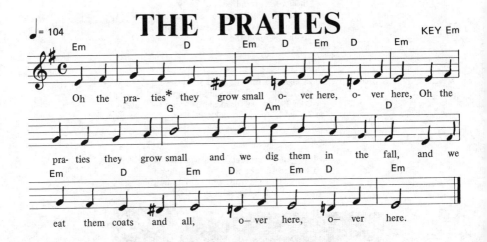

Oh the pra- ties* they grow small o- ver here, o- ver here, Oh the
pra- ties they grow small and we dig them in the fall, and we
eat them coats and all, o- ver here, o- ver here.

Oh I wish that we were geese, night and morn, night and morn
Oh I wish that we were geese and could live our lives in peace
Till the hour of our release, eating corn, eating corn

Oh we're down into the dust over here,
Oh we're down into the dust, but the Lord in whom we trust,
Will repay us crumb for crust, over here, over here.

potatoes

Searching for
potatoes during the
famine (*Illustrated
London News*,
22 December 1849)

52

FARE THEE WELL ENNISKILLEN

♩ = 152   KEY D

Fare thee well En- nis- kil- len, fare thee well for a
while, To all your fair wa- ters and eve- ry green
isle, Oh, your green isle will flou- rish your fair wa- ters
flow, While I from old Ire- land an ex- ile must go.

Her hair is as brown as the young raven's wing
Her eyes are as clear as the blue-bell of spring,
And light was her laugh like the sun on the sea
Till the weight of the world came between her and me.

Oh, what can a man do when the world is his foe,
And the look of her people fall on him like snow,
But bend the brow boldly and go away far,
To follow good fortune and get home in the war.

If the worst comes to worse, sure 'tis only to die,
And the true lass that loves me, can hold her head high;
Can hold her head high, though the fond heart may break,
For her lover lived bravely and died for her sake.

THE LIMERICK RAKE

♩. = 76

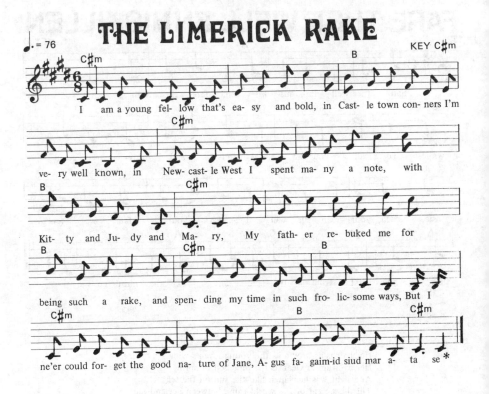

I am a young fel-low that's ea-sy and bold, in Cast-le town con-ners I'm ve-ry well known, in New-cast-le West I spent ma-ny a note, with Kit-ty and Ju-dy and Ma-ry, My fath-er re-buked me for being such a rake, and spen-ding my time in such fro-lic-some ways, But I ne'er could for-get the good na-ture of Jane, A-gus fa-gaim-id siud mar a-ta se *

My parents had reared me to shake and to mow,
To plough and to harrow, to reap and to sow,
But my heart being airy to drop it so low
I set out on high speculation.
On paper and parchment they taught me to write,
In Euclid and Grammar they opened my eyes,
And in Multiplication in truth I was bright,
Agus fagaimid siud mar ata se.

If I chance for to go to the town of Rathkeal,
The girls all round me do flock on the square,
Some give me a bottle and others sweet cakes,
To treat me unknown to their parents,
There is one from Askeaton and one from the Pike,
Another from Arda, my heart was beguiled,
Tho' being from the mountains her stockings are white,
Agus fagaimid siud mar ata se.

We'll leave it as it is.

ALTERNATIVE CHORDSHAPES :
Capo in fourth box
C#m = Am, B = G.

To quarrel for riches I ne'er was inclined,
For the greatest of misers must leave them behind,
I'll purchase a cow that will never run dry,
And I'll milk her by twisting her horn.
John Damer of Shronel had plenty of gold,
And Devonshire's treasure is twenty times more,
But he's laid on his back among nettles and stones,
Agus fagaimid siud mar ata se.

This cow can be milked without clover or grass,
For she's pampered with corn, good barley and hops
She's warm and stout, and she's free in her paps,
And she'll milk without spancel or halter.
The man that will drink it will cock his caubeen,
And if anyone coughs there'll be wigs on the green,
And the feeble old hag will get supple and free,
Agus fagaimid siud mar ata se.

If I chance for to go to the market at Croom,
With a cock in my hand and my pipes in full tune,
I am welcome at once and brought up to a room,
Where Bacchus is sporting with Venus.
There's Peggy and Jane from the town of Bruree,
And Biddy from Bruff and we all on the spree,
Such a combing of locks as there was about me,
Agus fagaimid siud mar ata se.

There's some say I'm foolish and more say I'm wise,
But being fond of the women I think is no crime,
For the son of King David had ten hundred wives,
And his wisdom was highly recorded.
I'll take a good garden and live at my ease,
And each woman and child can partake of the same,
If there's war in the cabin, theirselves they may blame,
Agus fagaimid siud mar ata se.

And now for the future I mean to be wise,
And I'll send for the women that acted so kind,
And I'll marry them all on the morrow by and by,
If the clergy agree to the bargain.
And when I'm on my back and my soul is at peace,
These women will crowd for to cry at my wake,
And their sons and their daughters will offer their prayer,
To the Lord for the soul of their father.

THE WILD COLONIAL BOY

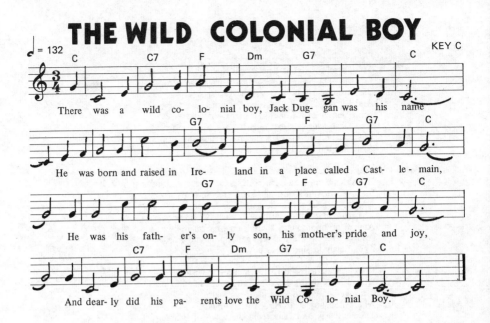

♩ = 132 KEY C

There was a wild co-lo-nial boy, Jack Dug-gan was his name

He was born and raised in Ire-land in a place called Cast-le-main,

He was his fath-er's on-ly son, his moth-er's pride and joy,

And dear-ly did his pa-rents love the Wild Co-lo-nial Boy.

At the early age of sixteen years he left his native home
And through Australia's sunny clime he was inclined to roam.
He robbed the lordly squatters, their flocks he would destroy
A terror to Australia was the Wild Colonial Boy.

For two long years this daring youth ran on his wild career,
With a heart that knew no danger, their justice did not fear.
He stuck the Beechworth coach up and he robbed judge McEvoy,
Who, trembling, gave his gold up to the Wild Colonial Boy.

He bade the judge 'Good morning' and he told him to beware
For he never robbed an honest judge what acted "on the square"
'Yet you would rob a mother of her son and only joy,
And breed a race of outlaws like the Wild Colonial Boy.

One morning on the prairie wild Jack Duggan rode along,
While listening to the mocking birds singing a cheerful song.
Out jumped three troopers fierce and grim, Kelly, Davis and FitzRoy,
They all set out to capture him, the Wild Colonial Boy.

'Surrender now, Jack Duggan, you can see there's three to one,
Surrender in the Queen's name, sir, you are a plundering son.
Jack drew two pistols from his side and glared upon FitzRoy,
'I'll fight, but not surrender ' cried the Wild Colonial Boy.

He fired point blank at Kelly and brought him to the ground,
He fired a shot at Davis too, who fell dead at the sound.
But a bullet pierced his brave young heart from the pistol of FitzRoy,
And that was how they captured him- the Wild Colonial Boy.

HUSH LITTLE BABY

♩ = 108

KEY G

G | D7 | G

Hush, lit- tle ba- by don't say a word, Mam- my's goin' to buy you a

G | D7 | G

mock-ing bird if that mock- ing bird don't sing Mam-my's goin' to buy you a dia-mond ring.

If that diamond ring turns brass
Mama's going to buy you a looking glass
If that looking glass gets broke
Mama's going to buy you a billy goat.

If that billy goat won't pull
Mama's going to buy you a cart and bull
If that cart and bull turn over
Mama's going to buy you a dog named Rover.

If that dog named Rover don't bark
Mama's going to buy you a horse and cart
If that horse and cart fall down
You're still the sweetest little girl in town.

all 'round my hat

♩ = 84　　　　　　　　　　　　　　　　　　　　　　　　　　KEY D

All 'round my hat, I will wear a green wil-low,
All 'round my hat for a twelve month and a day; If
a-ny-bo-dy asks me the rea-son why I wear it, it's
all be-cause my true love is far, far a-way.

My love she was fair and my love she was kind too
And many were the happy hours, between my love and me.
I never could refuse her, whatever she'd a mind to,
And now she's far away, far o'er the stormy sea.

Will my love be true and will my love be faithful,
Or will she find another swain to court her where she's gone.
The men will all run after her, so pretty and so graceful,
And leave me here lamenting, lamenting all alone.

All 'round my hat I will wear a green willow,
All 'round my hat for a twelve month and a day.
If anybody asks me the reason why I wear it,
It's all because my true love is far, far away.

MAIRI'S WEDDING

♩ = 100   KEY F

Step we gai- ly on we go, heel for heel and toe for toe,

Arm in arm and on we go, all for Mair- i's wed- ding.

O- ver hill- ways up and down, myrt- le green and brack- en brown

Past the shei- ling through the town, all for sake of Mair- i.

Plenty herring plenty meal
Plenty peat tae fill her creel
Plenty bonny bairns as weel
That's the toast for Mairi.

Cheeks as bright as rowans are
Brighter far than any star
Fairest of them all by far
Is my darling Mairi

Over hillways up and down
Myrtle green and bracken brown
Past the sheiling through the town
All for sake of Mairi.

THE BUTCHER BOY

♩ = 63   KEY C

In Lon-don town, where I did dwell, A butch-er boy I loved him well, He cour-ted me, for ma-ny a day, He stole from me, my heart a-way. I wish, I wish, I wish in vain, I wish I was a maid a-gain, A maid a-gain I ne'er can be, Till ap-ples grow on an i-vy tree.

There is an inn in that same town
And there my love he sits him down;
He takes a strange girl on his knee
And tells her what he woun't tell me.

The reason is I'll tell you why
Because she's got more gold than I
But gold will melt and silver fly
And in time of need be as poor as I.

I'll go upstairs and make my bed
'There's nothing to do' my mother said.
My mother she has followed me,
Saying ' What is the matter, my daughter dear'

'Oh mother dear, you little know
What pains and sorrows or what woe
Go get a chair and sit me down
With pen and ink I'll write all down.

Her father he came home that night
Enquiring for his heart's delight..
He went upstairs, the door he broke
He found her hanging on a rope.

He took a knife and cut her down
And in her bosom these lines he found:
'Oh what a foolish girl was I
To hang myself for a butcher's boy.

'Go dig my grave both wide and deep,
Put a marble stone at my head and feet
And on my grave place a turtle dove
To show the world that I died for love.

sally gardens

♩ = 76

KEY C

Down by the Sal- ly gar- dens, my love and I did meet, She
passed the Sal- ly gar- dens, with lit- tle snow- white feet, She
bid me : 'Take love ea- sy, as the leaves grow on the tree, But
I, be- ing young and fool- ish, with her did not a- gree.

In a field down by the river my love and I did stand
And on my leaning shoulder, she laid her snow-white hand
She bid me take life easy, as the grass grows on the weirs;
But I was young and foolish and now am full of tears.

Down by the sally gardens, my love and I did meet;
She passed the sally gardens, with little snow-white feet.
She bid me take love easy, as the leaves grow on the tree;
But I being young and foolish, with her did not agree.

Geo Bickham delin & sc.

62

THE PARTING GLASS

♩ = 120   KEY Dm

Oh, all the mo- ney e'er I had, I spent it in good com-pa- ny, And
all the harm I've e- ver done, a- las it was to none but me, And
all I've done for want of wit to mem'-ry now I can't re- call; So
fill to me the part- ing glass, Good- night and joy be with you all.

Oh, all the comrades e'er I had,
They're sorry for my going away,
And all the sweethearts e'er I had,
They'd wished me one more day to stay,
But since it falls unto my lot
That I should rise and you should not,
I gently rise and softly call,
Goodnight and joy be with you all.

If I had money enough to spend,
And leisure time to sit awhile,
There is a fair maid in this town,
That sorely has my heart beguiled.
Her rosy cheeks and ruby lips,
I own, she has my heart in thrall,
Then fill to me the parting glass,
Good night and joy be with you all.

Tom Carthy.
Who lived to the wonderful age of 105.
Irish Piper. Ballybunion, Co. Kerry.

63

notes on the songs

ALTHOUGH IN NO WAY MEANT TO BE COMPREHENSIVE, THE FOLLOWING NOTES WILL GIVE AS FAR AS IS RELEVANT AND TRACEABLE SOME IDEA OF THE BACKGROUND OF EACH SONG.

PAGE 1   THE RAGGLE TAGGLE GYPSIES

Originally this is a Scottish ballad also recorded in Devonshire and Ireland. In the Devon version it states that the lady was at first abducted by the Lord of Cassil and forced to marry against her will. The real event behind this ballad was the execution of Johnny Faa, a Scottish gypsy chieftain in 1624. In the Scots original Johnny ends up at the gallows, while the lady is found back by her husband. All later versions allow the lady to take off with the gypsies, never to be seen again. The same ballad may also be found under the titles of : The gypsie laddie, The dark-eyed gypsie, and in America as 'Black Jack Davy' or ' Gypsum Davy '. A popular updated Irish version written by Leo Maguire can be found in this volume on page 15 (The whistlin' Gypsy).

PAGE 2   THE SHORES OF AMERIKAY

Although obviously a recent song compared to the one above, apart from saying that the waltzey tune indicates a turn-of-the-century effort, nothing is known about its composer.

PAGE 3   PEGGY GORDON

This is one of a complete body of Scottish songs that found its way into Ireland and took root so firmly that if it wasn't for the obvious name of the lass, one might forget were it originally came from.

PAGE 4   I KNOW MY LOVE

Dr Douglas Hyde recalled hearing this song at a Galway Feis , with alternate verses in the Irish language. A longer version exists in Scotland. It is to be sung in a flowing manner without any pauses.

PAGE 5   THE HOLY GROUND

Although there did exist a seedy quarter of this name in the harbour town of Cobh, co Cork, it is more likely that Swansea in Wales can lay claim to this song. It dates from the last century when sailors diffused its rousing chorus to many a shore. Other versions are : 'Adieu my lovely Nancy', and 'Nancy of Yarmouth '. Originally this was a sea-shanty aiding the sailors with the various slow-paced actions aboard a sailing ship. The word shanty, like in shantytown, according to some, springs from a dark passage in Ireland's history. The story is that Cromwell deported about 5000 children from counties Kilkenny, Waterford and Sth Tipperary to sell them as young slaves in the plantations of the Barbadoes. The songs they sang may have been called ' songs of the old home ', sean tigh' in Irish. Phonetically this corresponds with 'shanty ' as we use it today, both for sailors action-songs and makeshift habitations. Although this theory may be correct in the case of the shanty dwellings I would find it easier to believe that the origins of the sailor's shanty may be found in the french words ' Chant ' and Chantez '.

PAGE 6   MRS MC GRATH

Together with 'Johnny I hardly knew yeh', one of the few realistic songs about the ravages and sickness of war. This was the most popular marching song of the Irish Volunteers in the years 1913-16.

PAGE 8   I'M A ROVER AND SELDOM SOBER

A Scottish bothy-ballad, the words are similar to ' The night visiting song', which in turns stems from ' The lover's ghost ' or ' The grey cock '. Too often this song is performed in a sort of a drinking-song manner, the lyrics deserve better than that.

One of the many transportation songs. Australia quickly found a new population with the English courts' vicious sentences which ripped families and communities apart in all parts of the empire, usually for crimes as trivial as poaching or the theft of a bread. Tasmanian whalers are known to have had a version of this song, 'The hat with the velvet band ', which served them as a working, drinking and fighting song.

The words are by Patrick Joseph Mc Call (1861-1919). The tune is alledged to have been played by Mac Hugh's pipers as he marched on Carlow after defeating the Lord Deputy Grey's troops at Glenmalure (1580).

Also known as 'The shoemaker '- was first reported in Sussex, Herefordshire and Dorset in around 1900. The lyrics were matched to various tunes. This version has recently gained popularity in Ireland.

Written by Thomas Davis (1814- 1845) a Dublin barrister, who with Daniel O'Connell, John Mitchell and others founded the Young Ireland Movement in 1842. The weekly paper published by them was called The Nation. Together with songs by Gavan Duffy and others, ' The West's Asleep ' was printed in a compilation of songs and ballads from The Nation in 1843. The tune used is a variant of ' Carrigdhoun '.

In the last century, in Limavady, co Derry, Jane Ross, a music collector heard a street musician play the air and subsequently gave it to George Petrie, who published it in his collection. It is said that the melody was composed by Rory Dall O' Cahan of Coleraine, chief harpist to Hugh O' Neill. Many different sets of lyrics have been applied to the tune since its discovery. Dr Joyce, an other collector from the last century , claimed the song was Irish and submits the following translation of the first stanza :
Would God I were a little apple
Or one of the small daisies
Or a rose in the garden
Where thou art accustomed to walk alone ;
In hope that thou wouldst pluck from me
Some wee little branch
Which thou wouldst hold in thy right hand
Or in the breast of thy robe

A.P. Graves, in 'Irish songs and ballads (1882)', uses these lines for a drawing room, Thomas Moore-type song : 'Love's wishes '. Other versions are : 'Would God I were the tender apple blossom' by Katherine Tynan, 'Acushla mine ' by Terry Sullivan, while the air itself became known as 'The Londonderry air '. Today's most widely sung version is from the hand of Fred F. Weatherly (1848- 1929) an Englishman who published a book of poems, translated Mascagni's 'Cavalleria Rusticana ' and the author of an other hit - 'Roses of Picardy '.

Written by Leo Maguire, this is really an up-tempo adaptation of the Scottish ballad 'The gypsy Laddie ' and ' The raggle taggle gypsies ' ; for further notes see under PAGE 1.

Colm O' Lochlainn learned this tune in 1925 in Dublin from a one-legged accordion player in Harcourt Street. The words have been found printed on a broadsheet, which was the common way of distributing songs until world-war II.

PAGE 18   AVONDALE
Charles Stuart Parnell (1846- 1891), a young protestant landowner, was born in Avondale house, a comfortable country mansion in co Wicklow. For a while partner of Michael Davitt, later president of the Land League and statesman extraordinary.

PAGE 19   NORA
Originally ' When you and I were young Maggie ', written by George W. Johnson, a Canadian teacher who married a Maggie Clark, a student of his in 1865. They moved to Cleveland Ohio, where Maggie died that same year. The song was published a year later. Music is by J.A. Butterfield (1837-1891), a violinist, singer and music teacher who settled in Chicago, where he started a publishing firm. This song is his one great success.

                            (from The Parlour Song Book)

Sean O'Casey uses this song in his play about the Easter uprising ' The plough and the stars ' :

> Nora : 'You haven't sung me a song since our honeymoon
> Sing me one now, do . . . . Please Jack !
> Clitheroe : 'What song ?, Since Maggie went away ' ?
> Nora : ' Ah, no , Jack, not that, it's too sad.
> When you said you loved me.

(Clearing his throat, Clitheroe thinks for a moment and then begins to sing Nora, putting an arm around him, nestles her head on his breast and listens delightfully).   Clitheroe : (singing verses following to the air of 'When you and I were young Maggie ')
> ' Th' violets were scenting th' woods, Nora'   etc.

PAGE 20   KELLY THE BOY FROM KILLANE
A song about the Wexford rising of 1798. John Kelly was a merchant's son from Killanne, co Wexford. After fighting at New Ross and Wexford he was captured by the English and hanged. The words are by P.J.Mc Call the author of ' Follow me up to Carlow. ' and ' Boulavogue'.

PAGE 22   THE BANKS OF THE OHIO
Joan Baez was one of many folksingers who made this old american song, which in itself derives from british broadsides, into the popular song it is today.

PAGE 23   MAIDS WHEN YOU'RE YOUNG
Also known as ' The old man came courting me ' this song is known in all english-speaking nations. Just like ' I'm a rover and seldom sober ' it is usually sung in a rowdy manner, while it deserves better.

PAGE 24   THE GALWAY RACES
Words are from a printed balladsheet of the last century. The same song was used at different races with the insertion of the relevant name of the venue.

PAGE 26   SAM HALL
In 1701, Jack Hall, a chimneysweep, was hanged for burglary. This event was used by C.W.Ross, an English comic minstrel man who composed and sang this song with great success in the London music halls of the 1850's.

PAGE 27   BOSTON CITY
This song appeared first as a broadside and set to various tunes eventually turned into a Strauss- sort of a tune. The 19th cent. craze for waltzing in fact affected a great many ballads that had up to that time been sung to traditional airs.

PAGE 28   THE NIGHTINGALE
An English song, although also widely recorded in Ireland, also known as ' The bold grenadier ', from a broadsheet.

PAGE 30   MY LAGAN LOVE
Words by Joseph Mc Cahill set to an ancient air. An American version of it is called ' The quiet joys of brotherhood '.

PAGE 31   I KNOW WHERE I'M GOING
A song from co Antrim. 'dear knows ' is Ulster dialect for : goodness knows.
'Black ': dour, ungracious.

PAGE 32   GLORY O TO OUR BOLD FENIAN MEN
Peadar Kearney was the author of several well-known songs of which the 'Soldiers Song , our National Anthem (1910) is obviously best known while he also turned his hand to writing parodies like : 'Fish and Chips' to the air of 'Down by the Slaney side '.

PAGE 33   CARRIGDHOUN
Percy French, or rather his arranger Collisson, used bits of this old air for 'The Mountains of Mourne '. Another celebrity using it was Tom Moore -' Bendermeer stream '. The song tells of Sarsfield's Wild Geese, who left the country in 1691. Words are by Corkman Denny Lane, who at first called it ' The lament of the Irish maiden '.

PAGE 34   VAN DIEMAN'S LAND
Abel Tasman and his aid Van Dieman were Dutch colonizers. Tasman gave his name to Tasmania, while Van Dieman's land became synonymous with Australia and transportation in general, to thousands of Irish,Scots and others. First printed on a broadsheet in 1830, this ballad appears in Ireland, Scotland, England, America and Australia.

PAGE 36   THE CURRAGH OF KILDARE
Taken down at different times by collectors like Petrie and Joyce, this song has been published with a set of lyrics known in Scotland and one of Irish origin, different airs were in use with this 18th cent. song.

PAGE 37   THE DRUNKEN SAILOR
This was the favourite 'runaway, or stamp and go ' shanty. Unlike other shanties, it required no soloists but was usually sung by all hands as they ran away with with the braces when swinging the yards round in tacking ship.
                        (from The Seven Seas Shanty Book)

PAGE 38   THE WELL BELOW THE VALLEY
A gruesome story, belonging to the moral-carrying body of ballads and even fairy-tales of medieval days. These songs and stories, apart from being mere entertainment also fulfilled an important role in moral, religeous and social education. This song was collected in Boyle, co Roscommon as an example of a basically English song that survived here in Ireland, while it is no longer current in its country of origin, It is another version of 'The woman and the palmer ', a popular account of the story of Jezus and the woman of Samaria, (John IV) A similar type ballad is : 'The cruel mother '.

PAGE 40   GOD SAVE IRELAND
This song written by T.D.O'Sullivan (1827- 1914), appeared in The Nation, on Dec 7 1867. The original note written by Sullivan himself runs as follows : Desirous of paying such tribute as I could to the memory of the patriots (Manchester Martyrs, Ed), I wrote, afew days after their execution, a song which had for its refrain the prayer which they had uttered in the docks, ' God save Ireland' With a view of getting it into immediate use, I fitted the words to a military air of American origin, 'Tramp, tramp, tramp the boys are marching ', which was popular at the time in Ireland. My intentions were fully realised ; on the day of its publication in The Nation - it was sung in the homes of Dublin working men, on the following day I heard it sung and chorused by a crowd of people in a railwaytrain at Howth . (T.D.O'Sullivan.: recollections of troubled times in Irish politics) The American original tune was by George F. Root, the song was used in America's civil war. God save Ireland was reprinted on broadsheets, sometimes under the title of 'The Manchester Patriot Martyrs '.

PAGE 42 THE CROPPY BOY
Myriads of versions of this song exist. The most commonly known one is given here. New Geneva (3rd verse) is near Passage, co Waterford, where a colony of Huguenots settled in 1783, but soon left for America. The British later used the place as a prison and torturehouse in 1798. The text of the song is from a contempory broadsheet printed by Haly in Cork city. This political ballad also appeared on the market with an entirely different set of words : 'Mc Caffery ', describing the downfall of an Irish private in the British army. There is a certain resemblance between the air used for The croppy boy ' and a popular Elizabethan lute -tune, used by Shakespeare called Callino Custurame . This,it is has been proven,was a garbled semi-phonetic adaptation of an old Irish song of the times ' Cailin O' Chois 't Siuire Me. Text and tune were published together in M.J. Murphy's 'National songs of Ireland ' 1892. It has also been collected under the title ' My boy Willie '.

PAGE 43 THE RIDDLE SONG
This is a dialogue-type song which can be traced back right to the 15th cent. An Oxford manuscript includes a ballad in which a maiden is accosted by the devil disguised as an earthling. To escape his power she has to solve the seemingly impossible riddles. Although so strange a theme to us now, all this is surely a reminder of pagan and early - christian times-. Right through to our times, when a song like Scarborough fair hits the charts - the riddle-type song remains as a testimony of the supernatural used in the people's folksong tradition. The version popular here today may have travelled back from America where it was first introduced by settlers from Britain.

PAGE 44 JOHNNY I HARDLY KNEW YEH
Music attributed to Patrick Gilmore. In the anon. poem of the same title, the reference to Ceylon (Sulloon) dates it to the early 19th cent. when a lot of Irishmen fought for the British to protect the East India Company.

PAGE 46 STILL I LOVE HIM
The tune hails from East Anglia, its first dtanza is used in an old English streetballad 'William an' Dinah ', later turned into ' Villikens and his Dinah', a variety hall song of the 1840's. The American folksong 'Sweet Betsy from Pike ' seems very similar too.

PAGE 47 THE ROAD TO DUNDEE
An Irish version of this lovely Scottish song may be found on page 14 of Vol III of this series.

PAGE 48 PLAISIR D'AMOUR (THE JOYS OF LOVE)
Made popular by Joan Baez and Nana Mouskouri. The second part of this through-composed art song has been cut here to use its first folk song-like stanza only. Music by Giovanni Battista, called Padre Martini, (1706- 1784), a Franciscan friar, learned musician and musical historian, composer and teacher of other composers. The original French words are by Florian, while the English translation is anonymous.

PAGE 49 THE HILLS OF CONNEMARA
Composer unknown , the first part of the tune is used in an English song, also well-known in America, : 'The keeper '.

PAGE 50 PADDY WORKS ON THE RAILWAY
Originally a sea-shanty, later adopted by landlubbers. Exists with a different air in the American repertoire. Also known as 'The Erie canal ', or ' Paddy works on the Erie'. Apart from the railroads, most of the subways and other gigantic undertakings in America, Irishmen also dug the Erie Canal.

PAGE 52 THE PRATIES
There was a partial famine in Ireland in 1845, a general one in 1846, and it was universal in 1847. Mass graves and starving peasants, who blocked themselves in their cottages to die unheard, unmissed , such was the scene in Ireland during that dreadful holocaust. With all this going on, the British administration at the time still saw fit to export food to England and to deport starving Irish peasants for the theft of a vegetable.

69

guitar accompaniments

For those who wish to use the Guitar-Accompaniments, I must stress the importance of learning those few extra chords that will break the 'three-chord trick' monotony.

Another thing to work on is the choosing of a key that actually suits your type of voice. A capo is handy enough in many cases but on the whole it is preferred to get a grasp of the idea of changing the key, (and with it the chords) of a song to transpose it into a key that really suits

You may substitute any of the keys indicated in the top-right hand corner of each song, for one that suits you according to your knowledge of chords and type of voice.

A table for transposing (changing) any key in this book and in fact any other book you may have, can be found on one of the last pages.

Finally, there is an infinite variety of right-hand strums and finger-picking styles available for the folk-guitarist, some of which can be learned from printed tutors although most are best demonstrated by a professional player or teacher.

Chords in brackets are optional and need not be played by beginning guitarists with no knowledge of bar-chords.

Metronome indication are equally optional but will be found of use to those who find themselves unfamiliar with certain songs.

In some songs, where the keys are physically difficult for guitar-players, reference is made to the use of a capo to simplify matters. The resulting different chords are indicated and may be pencilled in next to the original chords. The key of course, remains the same, unless you specifically want to use a higher or lower pitch, in which case the table of 'changing keys' in Volume 1 will be helpful.

IMPORTANT NOTE :

Rather than indicating each CHORUS separately and between each verse, throughout the book the beginning of a CHORUS is marked thus : ⌐──   If present, the chorus will be repeated after each verse.

Folksongs & Ballads Popular in Ireland, by John Loesberg.
150 Irish songs in words, music & chords with interesting
notes on the history of each song. Volumes I, II , III.

The Roche Collection of Traditional Irish Music, by Frank
Roche. This new edition incorporates the original three
volumes with a new introduction & biography by Michael
O Suilleabhain. 566 Irish airs, marches & dance tunes suit-
able for most trad. instruments. 250 pages, sewn in signa-
tures, luxury cream paper. In Paperback & Hardback.

Irish pieces arranged for Guitar, by John Loesberg.
Vol I — Fourteen easy to moderately difficult pieces.
Vol II — Another fourteen pieces up to recital standard.

The Irish National Anthem, for Voice & easy Piano,
arranged by John Gibson. (in Irish & English).

**Music by Carolan, arranged for Recorder (flute, violin, oboe)
and Keyboard, with optional Bass part,** by Douglas Gunn.

**Traditional Irish Music arranged for Recorder (flute, violin,
oboe) and Keyboard,** by Douglas Gunn.

Suite of Irish Airs arranged for Piano, by T.C. Kelly.

Irish Song & Balladsheets in Posterform, 12 different sheets
in three colours on luxury ivory paper, ready for framing.

Opus One, a piano tutor for all beginners , by Nina Dalby.

The Songs of Eric Bogle, 24 of the best songs of the author
of : The Band played Waltzing Mathilda, The Green Fields
of France, Leaving Nancy, etc.

Geraldine Cotter's Traditional Irish Tin Whistle Tutor.
The definitive book on Irish tin whistle playing, with an
appendix of 100 choice Irish tunes and an instruction record
included, spiral binding.
